herbs & spices

Published by
Tesco Stores Limited
Created by Brilliant Books Ltd
84-86 Regent Street
London W1B 5RR

First published 2000
ISBN 1-84221-103-X

Text and Illustrations © 2000 Brilliant Books Ltd
Printed by Printer Trento S.r.l., Italy
Reproduction by Colourpath, England

10 9 8 7 6 5 4 3 2 1

herbs
& spices

Written by
Jo Younger

introduction

This inspiring book is packed with new ideas on how to cook with herbs and spices creatively. It describes how to recognise, choose, prepare and use all the culinary herbs and spices from allspice to vanilla.

The quick and easy recipes show how herbs and spices can lift a dish from the plain and ordinary to the exotic. Just think of the unmistakable flavour of fresh basil, the exciting kick of chillies and the golden colour of saffron.

As well as individual herbs and spices, the wide range of special blends of herbs and seasonings now available makes it even easier to give a favourite dish a new twist.

Storage

Dried herbs and spices will keep for up to 12–18 months
if stored properly. Whole spices should keep for up to
three years. To keep herbs and spices at their best:

• Store in airtight glass jars in a cool, dry, dark place.
• Keep fresh herbs wrapped in a damp clean cloth, or
  in damp kitchen paper, in the fridge. Always use as fresh
  as possible for the maximum flavour.
      • Try preserving herbs and spices in oils and
        vinegars and use these in your cooking,
        sauces and salad dressings.

allspice

Imagine the flavours of cinnamon, nutmeg, cloves and black pepper all rolled into one and you have the exotic taste of allspice. This little berry is one of the most versatile spices, excellent used in both sweet and savoury dishes.

Allspice is the dried, unripe berry of the allspice tree. It looks very much like a large reddish-brown peppercorn. Although you can buy allspice whole or ground, it is best to buy it whole and grind it yourself. When ground, allspice has a pungent scent and tastes both sweet and sharp.

Culinary uses

Allspice adds a warm spiciness to cakes and puddings, it is an essential ingredient in pickling spice and it is used in marinades for meat, game and fish. In India and the West Indies it flavours curries and rice dishes.

- Try allspice, salt, sugar, pepper and wine poured over grilled salmon.
- Schwartz Jamaican Jerk Seasoning is a warm blend of allspice, chilli powder, onion, garlic and other seasonings – delicious rubbed on to pork or chicken that is marinated, then grilled or barbecued.
- Add a pinch of ground allspice to a fruit-crumble topping.

Did you know...?

- Allspice can be used to relieve some digestive problems such as flatulence and diarrhoea.
- The oil is used in many men's perfumes and soaps.
- In the West it is a traditional ingredient of pot pourri.

Serves 4

Preparation 20 mins

Cooking 2 hrs 15 mins

Calories 487

Fat 28g

3 tbsp olive oil

700g (1lb 9oz) stewing beef,
trimmed of fat and cut into
6cm (2½in) chunks

6 shallots, finely chopped

2 garlic cloves, crushed

2 celery sticks, thickly sliced

300g (11oz) mushrooms,
thickly sliced

½ tsp ground allspice

½ bottle Rioja or other
full-bodied red wine

250ml (9fl oz) passata

2 sprigs fresh thyme

Salt and black pepper

Garlic mash, to serve

Spiced Spanish beef stew

1 Preheat the oven to 180°C/350°F/Gas Mark 4.
Heat the oil in a flameproof casserole dish, add
the meat and fry over a high heat, stirring, for 5–10
minutes, until browned. Remove from the pan, then
add the shallots, garlic and celery. Cook, stirring,
for 3–4 minutes, until lightly browned.

2 Add the mushrooms and cook for 1 minute or
until softened. Stir in the allspice, wine, passata,
1 sprig of thyme and season. Return the meat to
the dish or pan and bring the mixture to a simmer.

3 Cover and cook in the centre of the oven or on a
low heat on the hob for 1½–2 hours, until the beef is
tender. Check the seasoning, then serve garnished
with the remaining thyme and garlic mash.

Serves 4

Preparation 10 mins

Cooking 15 mins

Calories 273

Fat 18g

4 tbsp olive oil

1 tsp dried mixed herbs

Black pepper

1 French white bread stick,

cut into 12 slices

8 plum tomatoes

1 garlic clove, crushed

25g (1oz) sun-dried

tomatoes in oil, drained

and finely chopped

1 tsp vinegar

1 tsp sugar

2 tbsp chopped fresh basil

Tomato & basil toasts

1 Preheat the oven to 220°C/425°F/Gas Mark 7.
Combine 3 tablespoons of the oil with the mixed
herbs and season well. Brush both sides of each
bread slice with the flavoured oil. Cook the toasts
on a baking tray for 8 minutes or until lightly
golden and crisp on both sides.

2 Meanwhile, put the tomatoes in a large bowl,
cover with boiling water and leave for 30 seconds.
Peel and deseed, then roughly chop the flesh.

3 Heat the remaining olive oil in a frying pan and add
the garlic, chopped tomatoes, sun-dried tomatoes,
vinegar, sugar and basil. Cook, stirring occasionally,
for 5 minutes, until heated through. Pile the tomato
mixture on top of the toasts, season and serve.

basil

The intense flavour of basil, with its warm, spicy scent makes it one of the finest culinary herbs, much loved by the Italians and a familiar ingredient in Italian cookery – think of pasta with pesto, and tomato and mozzarella salad with fresh basil.

The pungent scent and distinctive flavour of basil have become familiar and well-loved elements of many dishes today, especially in Italian cookery. It can lift a basic recipe from bland and tasteless into something quite sensational. Not only does it boast great culinary benefits, basil also has many medicinal roles, from an aphrodisiac to a migraine remedy, from a natural antiseptic to a remedy for depression, stress and fatigue. There are over 100 varieties of basil, in many different colours, sizes, scents and tastes. The most popular and most commonly found is sweet basil with its small, soft, bright green leaves; but you can also find black basil with deep purple leaves and a powerful flavour, and the large-leafed variety from Naples, whose great leaves are a brilliant green, with a punchy, quite spicy flavour. This is the preferred basil for making pesto. Originally grown in India, where it is considered

Did you know...?

- Naturopaths maintain that an infusion of dried basil can help migraines, insomnia, nervous tension and even constipation.
- Traditionally, gargling with a basil infusion was prescribed to help alleviate sore throats.
- Crushed leaves or oil was often used to soothe wasp stings.

a holy plant, basil is now grown in many countries, from Europe (especially the Mediterranean) to Asia and America. When using basil, it is best to shred or tear the leaves with your fingers, as chopping not only spoils the flavour, it turns the leaves black at the edges as it bruises them. Basil is also best added to dishes after cooking or sprinkled on to cold food, such as salads and chilled soups, as the oils are highly volatile and the wonderful flavour spoils quickly when heated.

Culinary uses

Basil has a great affinity with tomatoes, as well as sweet peppers and aubergines and all those sweet Mediterranean vegetables. It is the perfect partner to eggs, fish (mostly white fish), green vegetables and bland cheeses, such as mozzarella, as in the classic tomato and mozzarella salad with basil. It also makes an excellent addition to salads, soups, pizza and pasta sauces.

• Make your own pesto by pounding fresh basil with Parmesan, pine nuts, garlic and olive oil and serve simply with spaghetti, or spread on to toasts, or use as a topping for roasted vegetables.

• Bake whole baby courgettes and chopped tomatoes in olive oil, then sprinkle with plenty of chopped fresh basil.

• Try adding 1–2 teaspoons of dried basil to tomato sauce and chilled soups such as gazpacho.

• Sprinkle basil on to pizzas and pasta, along with oregano, for a really authentic Italian flavour.

• Sprinkle a mixture of basil, salt, cumin and coriander on to lamb chops before grilling them.

• Make a herb butter with fresh or dried basil and garlic, and spread on to French bread and bake, to make delicious herby garlic bread.

bay leaf

Also known as Sweet bay and Sweet laurel, this handsome dark green leaf with its strong, distinctive taste is an important ingredient in the classic bouquet garni along with parsley and thyme, and is an essential flavouring for casseroles and stocks.

The bay tree is small and evergreen with oval-shaped, tough, glossy green leaves that have an astringent, spicy flavour. They can be used fresh or dried, although dried bay leaves are slightly less bitter than fresh. To release the volatile oils in the dried leaf, it is best to tear or break it before adding to your cooking and then remove before serving. The strength and flavour of bay leaves increases with cooking time, so add them at the start of cooking for maximum impact.

Culinary uses

Bay leaves are good in casseroles, stews, soups, sauces, stock, gravy, minced beef and even in sweet milk puddings.

• Ground bay leaves add extra flavour to Italian Bolognese sauce and other hearty minced-meat dishes.

• Try infusing milk with a bay leaf and adding to creamy rice pudding.

Did you know...?

• An infusion of bay leaves helps to stimulate the appetite and can be used as a digestive aid.

• Rubbing your body with oil infused with essence of bay can help ease many muscular aches and pains.

Serves 4

Preparation 15 mins

Cooking 30 mins

Calories 456

Fat 9g

500g pack fresh tagliatelle
For the tomato sauce
2 tbsp vegetable or olive oil
1 medium onion,
peeled and chopped
2 garlic cloves, peeled
and finely chopped
2 x 400g cans
chopped tomatoes
1 tsp sugar
1 bay leaf
1 tsp Schwartz Spicy
Italian Pasta
Sauce Seasoning
Salt and black pepper

Pasta & spicy tomato sauce

1 To make the sauce, heat the oil in a medium-sized heavy-based saucepan over a medium heat. Fry the onion, stirring occasionally, for 2 minutes or until slightly softened. Add the garlic and cook, stirring from time to time, for a further 3 minutes, until the onion is tender, but not coloured.

2 Add the tomatoes with the sugar and bay leaf. Bring to the boil and add the seasoning and salt and pepper. Reduce the heat, partly cover the pan and simmer, stirring occasionally, for 20 minutes until the sauce has thickened. Remove the bay leaf.

3 Meanwhile, cook the pasta according to packet instructions until al dente. Drain the pasta and serve with the sauce poured on top.

13

caraway seed

Caraway, with its distinctive, quite pungent taste, is a favourite flavouring in Austrian and German cooking, and is much used in rye breads, cakes and pastries, but it's best known here as a flavouring for good old-fashioned British seed cake.

Caraway seed is the dried fruit of a herb that is a member of the parsley family and is one of the world's oldest culinary spices. A small greeny-brown, ribbed seed, it looks very similar to cumin and is often confused with this spice, with its warm, pungent, slightly bitter flavour with a hint of anise, fennel and dill. It was once a very popular spice in England, especially in Elizabethan times when it was used in cakes, pastries and bread and with fruit, but today it is more often associated with German and Austrian foods, both in sweet and savoury dishes. Caraway is also used in children's medicines and mouthwashes and is great for freshening the breath. Always use caraway sparingly, however, as it can be an overpowering flavour if overused.

Culinary uses

Caraway works well with cabbage, pork, potatoes, onions and carrots, and can enliven coleslaw, sauerkraut, goulash, dumplings and many cheeses, pickles, cakes, biscuits and breads.

- Stir 1 tablespoon of caraway seeds into a plain sponge-cake mixture.
- Cook carrots with lemon juice, sugar, caraway seeds and butter.
- Stir-fry thinly sliced white cabbage with caraway seeds.
- Sprinkle lightly on to breads, cakes and pastries just before baking.

cardamom

One of the most ancient spices known, and called the 'queen of spices', the warm, slightly lemony flavour of cardamom is widely used in India and is one of the main ingredients in garam masala. Cardamom enhances many sweet dishes, too.

Cardamom is the dried, unripened fruit of a bush related to the ginger family. It is the slightly sticky seeds, crowded within a papery pod that contain all the flavour, which is highly aromatic, almost citrus-like. The pod can be green, white or brown and hairy, but the best seeds are from the green cardamom. Only the seeds are edible – the outer green pod is not eaten. Either crush the pods lightly and discard after cooking, or remove the seeds and use whole or ground.

Culinary uses

Cardamom can be used to flavour fish, meat, curries, rice, pickles, pastries, meringues, cream, yogurt, fruit, even tea and coffee.

- Flavour sugar-syrup with cardamom and pour over fruit salad.
- Use it in curries and Moroccan stews.
- Use ground cardamom in pastries, custards and ice cream.

Did you know...?

- Naturopaths claim that cardamom can assist digestion and can also relieve headaches.

- Cardamom infused in milk was a traditional cure for impotency.
- Chewing cardamom seeds disguises the smell of alcohol.

Serves 4

Preparation 25 mins

Cooking 30 mins

Calories 406

Fat 9g

3 plum tomatoes

25g (1oz) butter

1 large onion, sliced
lengthways

2 carrots, cut in half
lengthways, then
sliced diagonally

2 celery sticks, sliced

300g (11oz) pumpkin,
deseeded, or swede,
cut into 2cm (¾in) cubes

1 green pepper, deseeded
and chopped

½ tsp dried crushed chillies

300ml (½ pint) good quality
vegetable stock

400g (14oz) couscous

400g can chickpeas or
broad beans, drained

Salt and black pepper

Spicy vegetable couscous

1 Immerse the tomatoes in a bowl of boiling water
for 30 seconds. Peel, deseed and roughly chop.

2 Melt the butter in a large saucepan and fry the
onion, carrots, celery, pumpkin or swede and
pepper for 3–4 minutes, stirring, until softened.
Add the chillies and tomatoes, cover and cook for
5 minutes, shaking the pan occasionally. Add the
stock, cover and simmer for 20 minutes or until all
the vegetables are tender.

3 Meanwhile, prepare the couscous according to
the packet instructions. Stir the chickpeas or broad
beans into the vegetables, season, then simmer for
5 minutes or until warmed through. Serve the
vegetables piled on top of the couscous.

chillies

Chilli, otherwise known as the 'hot' spice, is popular all over the world in its many different forms, colours, shapes and sizes. It jazzes up even the most bland of dishes and is vital in Indian, Thai, South-East Asian, African and Mexican cookery.

Chillies are the pods of a plant related to the capsicum family that originated in Central and South America, but are now grown all over the tropics. There are more than 200 identified varieties of chilli – big ones, small ones, lantern-shaped ones and long, tall, thin ones. They can range from the very mild to fiery hot in flavour. The hottest chillies are generally the smaller, pointier ones, although there are exceptions to every rule. Only by experimenting with the various types of chilli available will you discover their heat levels, and how much you add to a recipe depends very much on how hot you like it. It is best to assume that a chilli is hot and proceed with caution; you can always add more according to taste. Chillies are great fun to use, adding colour, spice and heat to many bland dishes. You can buy chillies fresh, dried or crushed and in powder, paste, sauces and oils, as well as pickled.

Did you know...?

- Chillies are an excellent source of beta carotene and vitamin C.
- Chillies stimulate the saliva glands and can aid digestion.
- Chillies can help to clear a blocked nose and a 'stuffy' head.
- Some herbalists claim that the 'chilli high' you get from eating hot chillies can ease depression.

Cayenne pepper is pure ground chilli powder, also known as red pepper. As the majority of the heat in a chilli comes from the seeds and membranes, to reduce the heat, carefully remove the seeds and membrane before cooking. And remember – the longer chillies are cooked for, the hotter the dish will become. Dried whole chillies should be a deep rich-red colour and fairly pliable – add one to whatever you are cooking and then simply remove it before serving. Bananas and dairy foods, rice and bread are the best things to neutralise the effects of eating a hot chilli. Drinking water will simply prolong the agony.

Culinary uses

Chillies are widely used in Indian, Mexican, South-East Asian, Thai and Chinese Sichuan cookery – dishes such as curry, chilli con carne and satay all rely on chillies for their hot, spicy taste.

• Try making your own harissa sauce, a fiery-hot red sauce widely used in Moroccan cookery that is made from red chillies and other spices.

• Add crushed chillies to a stir-fry to give a piquant bite.

• Experiment with the wonderfully spicy and flavoursome red and green curries of Thailand, in which red or green chillies form the basis of the tasty curry pastes that give the curries their name.

• Add finely chopped chilli to tomato sauces for a nice spicy kick.

• Cayenne pepper can be used sparingly as a seasoning in savoury biscuits and in cheese and egg dishes.

Warning

Avoid touching your eyes after handling chillies as the capsaicin, the substance that gives them their fiery taste, really makes them sting.

Always wear rubber gloves when preparing fresh chillies.

chives

The mild, fresh onion flavour and bright green colour of chives make them a decorative and tasty addition to many dishes, such as omelettes, salads and potatoes, while in cream sauces, butters and cheeses they impart a lovely delicate flavour.

Chives are the green reed-like stems of a plant that is the smallest member of the onion family. Along with parsley, tarragon and chervil, they're an important ingredient in the *fines herbes* mixture used in French cooking. It's easier to cut chives with scissors than to chop them with a knife, which is why recipes usually refer to them as 'snipped'. Because the oils are highly volatile, add chives to cooked dishes at the last minute to preserve their delicate oniony flavour.

Culinary uses

Chives are good with cheese, salads, soups, fish and chicken, and make an excellent garnish for many dishes. They also add interest to bland food such as omelettes, cottage cheese and potatoes. They come into their own in cold dishes – think of potato salad with chives.

- They are perfect as a garnish for all types of salad.
- Mix them with soured cream for a yummy topping for jacket potatoes.
- Add chives to cream cheese as a filling for sandwiches.
- Use Schwartz Onion and Chive Mashed Potato Seasoning for adding great flavour to simple mashed potato.
- Chive butter, made by beating snipped chives and lemon juice into softened butter, is good melted on to grilled fish or meats.

20

Serves 4

Preparation 15 mins

Cooking 15 mins

Calories 446

Fat 33g

4 pieces smoked haddock
fillet, about 175g (6oz) each
250g bag fresh spinach,
stalks removed
Salt and black pepper
For the sauce
3 shallots, finely chopped
6 tbsp dry white wine
6 tbsp white wine vinegar
150g (5oz) unsalted butter
3 tbsp snipped fresh chives

Haddock & chive butter sauce

1 To make the sauce, place the shallots, wine and
5 tablespoons of the vinegar in a saucepan. Boil for
5–10 minutes to reduce the liquid to 1 tablespoon.
Strain, discard the shallots, then return the liquid
to the pan and set aside.

2 Place the fish, skin-side down, in a large
saucepan. Just cover with cold water and add the
remaining vinegar. Bring to a simmer, cover, then
remove from the heat and set aside.

3 Boil the spinach for 3 minutes until wilted. Drain
well and season. Heat the reserved wine liquid, then
whisk in the butter, until creamy. Add the chives and
season. Drain the fish, arrange on plates with the
spinach, then drizzle over the chive butter sauce.

Serves 6

Preparation 10 mins

Cooking 40 mins

Calories 424

Fat 24g

3 x 410g cans peach halves
in natural juice
3 pieces stem ginger
in syrup, drained and
finely chopped
100g (3½oz) plain flour
100g (3½oz) roasted
chopped hazelnuts
4 tbsp soft light brown sugar
1 tsp ground cinnamon
100g (3½oz) butter, cubed

Peach & hazelnut crumble

1 Preheat the oven to 200°C/400°F/Gas Mark 6.
Drain the peaches, reserve 200ml (7fl oz) of the
juice and set aside.

2 Carefully arrange the peaches, cut-side up, in
a 30 x 25cm (12 x 10in) ovenproof dish. Sprinkle the
ginger over. Boil the reserved juice in a saucepan
for 5 minutes or until reduced by one-third. Pour
the juice over the peaches.

3 In a large bowl mix together the flour, hazelnuts,
sugar and cinnamon. Add the butter and rub in with
the tips of your fingers until the mixture resembles
fine breadcrumbs. Sprinkle over the fruit and bake
for 30–35 minutes, until browned. Serve with a
dollop of fresh double cream, yogurt or custard.

cinnamon

With its exotic, warm, sweet and fragrant flavour, cinnamon is often associated with cakes, pastries and puddings and especially with Christmas recipes. It lends a distinct aroma and fabulous flavour to many savoury dishes, too.

The peeled, curled inner bark from the slim, young stems of a tropical evergreen tree that grows in Sri Lanka and other Far Eastern countries, cinnamon has a wonderful warm, sweet, woody aroma. The cinnamon sticks can be used whole to flavour liquids and sauces, or powdered. Cinnamon sticks should be an even, soft brown colour – whole sticks have only a faint aroma, but once broken or ground, the volatile oils are released giving off their powerfully pungent, sweet flavour.

Culinary uses

Cinnamon is perfect with beef, pork and spinach; it enlivens savoury and sweet rice dishes, pickles, cakes, biscuits, puddings, stewed fruits, mulled wine and chocolate. It's also an important ingredient in garam masala, the Indian blend of warm spices used in curries.

• Cinnamon sticks can be added whole to casseroles, rice dishes and mulled wine, then removed before serving.

• Add cinnamon to enhance chocolate recipes and drinks, and stir hot chocolate drinks with a cinnamon stick, as they do in Mexico.

• Add ground cinnamon to biscuits, fruit cakes and desserts.

• To make cinnamon toast, toast bread on one side, butter the other side, sprinkle with cinnamon and sugar, and toast until golden.

cloves

This aromatic spice, which distinctly resembles a small brown nail (the word clove comes from the French clou, meaning nail), is included in many classic spice mixtures, including Chinese five spice powder and ground mixed spice.

Cloves are the dried, unopened flowerbuds of a small evergreen tree that originated in Indonesia. They are picked when green, then dried until they turn brown and woody. They have a very strong, sweet, pungent flavour and can be overpowering – a little goes a long way. They are famously used as a flavouring in pickles and spiced dishes.

Culinary uses

Cloves are good with ham, gammon, onions and rice, and also have a special affinity with apples. Use them to flavour cakes, biscuits, desserts, mulled wine, and Chinese and Indonesian dishes.

• Add whole cloves to mulled wine with cinnamon sticks and coriander seeds, or warm Irish whiskey with cloves, lemon juice and sugar.

• An onion studded with one or two cloves gives steak and kidney pie and beef casseroles a warm, full flavour.

Did you know...?

• Clove oil is used in a huge variety of perfumes, in soaps and in some medicines.

• Applied externally to the area, clove oil can ease many aches and pains, but it's best known as a cure for toothache.

Serves 8–10

Preparation 15 mins
plus 3 hrs soaking

Cooking 1 hr 50 mins

Calories 441

Fat 19g

2kg (4lb 8oz) unsmoked
gammon joint, soaked in
cold water for 3 hours,
then drained
1 onion
20 whole cloves
1 tbsp black peppercorns
1 bouquet garni
300ml (½ pint) dry white wine
2 tbsp clear honey
2 tbsp Dijon mustard
Cumberland sauce, to serve

Roast ham with cloves

1 Place the gammon in a large saucepan. Stud the onion with some of the cloves and add to the pan with the peppercorns, bouquet garni and wine. Pour in enough cold water to cover the gammon, bring to the boil, then simmer, partly covered, for 1¼ hours.

2 Preheat the oven to 200°C/400°F/Gas Mark 6. Melt the honey and mustard in a small saucepan. Place the gammon in a roasting tin, and cut away the skin and all but a thin layer of fat. Score the remaining fat in a diamond pattern, brush with the honey mixture and stud with the remaining cloves. Roast for 30 minutes until the meat is cooked and the glaze is golden. Carve the ham in thin slices and serve, hot or cold, with Cumberland sauce.

coriander leaf

Coriander, with its bright green, feathery leaves, and distinctly aromatic flavour, is the familiar ingredient of Asian, Oriental, Middle Eastern and Latin American dishes. It is also creeping into many more European and Mediterranean recipes.

The flavour of the coriander leaf is strong, pungent, earthy and slightly spicy, quite different from the more aromatic, citrus flavour of the coriander seed. It is usually either loved or hated because the flavour is so pungent. It looks very like flatleaf parsley and has become an essential ingredient in modern British cooking or fusion-style food.

Culinary uses

Coriander complements chicken, fish, curries, rice, tomatoes, and Chinese, Indonesian, Thai and South American dishes. It can be used as a garnish in place of parsley, and in pesto as a substitute for basil.

• Coriander is an essential ingredient of Mexican salsa: simply combine chopped tomatoes, onion, garlic and crushed chillies with 1 tablespoon of chopped coriander leaf.

• For an Indian raita, stir chopped or grated cucumber, coriander leaf, salt and pepper into natural yogurt.

• A Thai-style fresh chutney makes an excellent accompaniment to grilled fish: warm creamed coconut with lemon juice and stir in fresh coriander leaves, crushed chillies and chopped spring onions.

• Add coriander leaf to breads, stuffings and sauces and sprinkle over spicy or creamy dishes at the end of cooking.

coriander seed

With its mild, sweet, citrus-like flavour, with a hint of sage, coriander seed adds a delicious zing to many dishes of the Middle East, South-East Asia and India. It is also used extensively in curry powders such as garam masala.

The seed is the dried, ripe fruit of the coriander plant. You can buy the seeds whole or ground. If whole, the seed should be a uniform light brown colour, even in size, and unblemished. Both the seeds and leaves are used in cooking, but they aren't interchangeable as they do have distinctly different flavours.

Culinary uses

Coriander seed adds spark to pork, lamb and many vegetables, to curries, lentils, chutney, pickles, stewed fruit, cakes and biscuits.

• Ground coriander and cumin together add taste to vegetables such as spinach, and to yogurt dressings and lassi.

• Try crushing the seeds to a paste with chopped parsley and olive oil and rubbing into lamb before roasting.

• Add ground coriander to carrot and orange soup.

• Ground coriander or crushed seeds both go well with fruit crumbles, especially apple and rhubarb crumbles.

• Eastern recipes often contain coriander seed; *baharat*, a seasoning blend from the Middle East, contains a heady mixture of coriander, nutmeg, cumin, cloves, cinnamon, cardamom, paprika and chilli, and is used extensively to spice both meat and vegetables.

Serves 4
Preparation 15 mins
plus 1 hr marinating
Cooking 10 mins
Calories 350
Fat 21g

500g (1lb 2oz) lamb leg
steaks, cut into
2.5cm (1in) pieces
125g (4oz) ready-to-eat
dried apricots
1 tbsp finely chopped
fresh mint
Salt and black pepper
1 lemon, cut into 8 wedges
For the marinade
1 garlic clove, crushed
2 tbsp low-fat natural yogurt
1 tbsp olive oil
1 tsp ground cumin
1 tsp ground coriander
1 tsp paprika
Pinch of cayenne pepper
Juice of 1 lemon

Lamb & apricot kebabs

1 To make the marinade, place the garlic, yogurt,
oil, cumin, coriander, paprika, cayenne and lemon
juice in a large non-metallic bowl and mix together.
Add the lamb, turning to coat. Cover and place in
the fridge for 1 hour to marinate. Wooden skewers
should be placed in water to soak for 10 minutes.

2 Stir the apricots and mint into the lamb and
season. Thread the meat and apricots on to eight
metal or wooden skewers, securing them with a
lemon wedge at both ends. Discard the marinade.

3 Preheat the grill to high. Place the kebabs on
a baking sheet under the grill and cook for 8–10
minutes, turning occasionally, until the meat has
browned. Spoon over the juices and serve.

Serves 4

Preparation 15 mins

Cooking 45 mins

Calories 116

Fat 4g

1 tbsp olive oil

1 large onion, chopped

1 garlic clove, crushed

3 celery sticks, chopped

1 tbsp ground cumin

700g (1lb 9oz) carrots,
thinly sliced

900ml (1½ pints) good quality
vegetable stock

Black pepper

Fresh coriander, to garnish

Cumin-spiced carrot soup

1 Heat the oil in a large saucepan, add the onion,
garlic and celery and fry gently for 5 minutes or until
softened, stirring occasionally. Add the cumin and
fry, stirring, for 1 minute to release its flavour.

2 Add the carrots, stock and black pepper to the
onion mixture and stir to combine. Bring to the boil
and simmer, covered, for 30–35 minutes, until the
vegetables are tender, stirring occasionally.

3 Remove the pan from the heat and cool for a few
minutes. Purée the soup until smooth in a food
processor or liquidiser, or with a hand blender.
Return the soup to a clean pan and reheat gently.
Garnish with fresh coriander leaves and serve with
some warmed naan bread on the side.

cumin

No curry powder would be complete without the distinctive, mildly spicy and slightly bitter taste of cumin seed. It is an incredibly adaptable spice, wonderful with beans, lentils and vegetables. It is the heart of many North African dishes.

Cumin is the aromatic seed of an umbrella-shaped plant similar to cow-parsley. Originally from the Middle East, it's now a popular spice throughout the East, Mexico, North Africa and India. In fact, the rich, spicy flavour of many of these countries' dishes is owing to the unique flavour of cumin. The seed is small, ridged and greeny-brown in colour and has an earthy, pungent, aromatic flavour that is very distinctive and slightly bitter, so not everyone takes to it immediately. Coriander seed, with which it's frequently combined, counteracts the bitterness. Lightly dry-roasting the seeds enhances their unique flavour and aroma.

Culinary uses

Cumin is excellent with chicken, lamb, cheese, vegetables, couscous, rice, lentil dhals, curries, Mexican dishes, tomato sauce and bread. It is an essential ingredient in curry powders and other blends such as garam masala, and is often used in rye bread.

- Dry-roast cumin seeds before using in dhal or bean soup.
- Use it to spice up vegetables and vegetable stews.
- It's one of the seasonings in falafel – fried balls of puréed chickpeas, a popular street food in the Middle East.
- Flavour chilli con carne, nachos, tacos and couscous with cumin.

31

dill weed

Dill is most famous for its use in the renowned Scandinavian marinated salmon dish of gravadlax. The feathery leaves of dill weed have a fresh, sweet, aniseed-like flavour. Seemingly made for salmon, it also enhances new potatoes, eggs and cream.

Dill weed is the leaf of a plant belonging to the parsley family, and looks so similar to fennel it could easily be confused with it, bearing feathery leaves and little yellow flowers. However, the flavour is very different to fennel, quite distinctive and aromatic, a little like parsley. It can also be substituted for parsley, mint or tarragon. Originally from southern Russia and the Mediterranean, it is now cultivated and used throughout Europe. It's best added mere moments before the end of cooking for the full flavour to be appreciated. It is also excellent in cold dishes.

Culinary uses

Dill weed is good with chicken, fish, vegetables, eggs, cheese, salads, soups, pickles and soured cream, and makes a refreshing garnish. It's used to flavour baby cucumbers in dill pickles and is an exquisite seasoning for seafood, fish and new potatoes served hot or cold. It is a common element of Scandinavian or central European cuisines.

• Dill weed is delicious in delicately flavoured sauces or butters.

• For a coleslaw-style salad, mix together minced onion, diced celery and shredded white cabbage, and toss in a dressing of soured cream, freshly squeezed lemon juice and dill weed.

• Use dill as an alternative to parsley in omelettes, quiches and salads.

Dill-crusted salmon

1 Preheat the oven to 200°C/400°F/Gas Mark 6. Butter an ovenproof dish. In a small heavy-based saucepan heat the butter and oil, then fry the onion and ginger, stirring occasionally, for 10 minutes to soften the onion. Add the anchovies and cook for 2 minutes until they are broken down. Purée in a food processor or using a hand blender, then mix in the almonds and matzo meal, dill and pepper.

2 Place the salmon steaks in the dish and spread the anchovy mixture on top. Cook for 10 minutes, then increase the heat to 230°C/450°F/Gas Mark 8. Cook for a further 8–10 minutes, until the salmon is cooked and the topping has browned. Serve with a fennel and orange salad and garnish with dill.

Serves 6
Preparation 20 mins
plus 30 mins chilling
Cooking 30 mins
Calories 564
Fat 38g

25g (1oz) butter,
plus extra for greasing
1 tbsp olive oil
1 onion, chopped
2.5cm (1in) piece fresh
root ginger, chopped
8 anchovy fillets, drained
and chopped
5 tbsp ground almonds
3 tbsp medium matzo meal
or fresh breadcrumbs
2 tbsp chopped fresh dill,
plus extra to garnish
Black pepper
6 salmon steaks, about
200g (7oz) each

fennel seed

Fennel seeds have been adopted in Mediterranean cookery for their sweet, aniseed-like flavour that goes particularly well with fish, as in the richly flavoured fish soups bouillabaisse and bourride. It's also an ingredient in some types of curry powder.

Fennel seeds are the dried, ripe fruit of a plant belonging to the parsley family. Once native to the Mediterranean, it is now grown worldwide. The oval, yellowish-brown seeds have a subtle, sweet flavour very like aniseed and are highly aromatic. The oil is used in drinks such as pastis and other anise-based drinks. In India fennel seed is chewed at the end of a meal to aid digestion and freshen the breath.

Culinary uses

Fennel complements fish, pork, veal, potatoes, rice, eggs, cheese, pickles and apples. In Italy fennel is used to season salmon and salami, in India fennel seeds are used in vegetarian dishes and in Iraq fennel is commonly used to flavour breads.

• It has a special affinity with fish, especially oily fish such as mackerel, herring and salmon – try adding it to the basting juices during cooking.

• Make a savoury dressing for grilled monkfish with crushed fennel seeds, olive oil, red wine vinegar, chopped onion and salt.

• Serve baked fish seasoned with fennel, lemon juice and dry white wine on a bed of pasta for a light summer supper.

• Add extra flavour to potato salad and rice dishes with crushed fennel seeds, and flavour risotto with fennel seeds and Parmesan.

fenugreek

With its strong aroma and bitter, curry-like flavour, fenugreek is mainly known as an ingredient of Indian curry powders, giving them their characteristic taste and distinctive smell. It is an important ingredient of many Indian and Sri Lankan dishes.

An annual herb belonging to the pea and bean family, fenugreek has pebbly, browny-yellow seeds with a strong, pungent taste. The seeds are rock hard, which is why they're always ground before use, and they should always be lightly toasted before grinding so as to mellow and draw out the flavour. However, if over-toasted, fenugreek becomes very bitter. Fenugreek needs long cooking to bring out its full flavour.

Culinary uses

Fenugreek is frequently used in Indian and Sri Lankan cookery, and is a familiar ingredient in curries, pickles and chutneys.

• Use it already incorporated in a variety of spice mixes, such as sambhar powder, which flavours southern Indian vegetable curries and dhal dishes, as well as some breads and batters.

• Experiment with it in Indian fish, meat and vegetable dishes.

Did you know...?

• Fenugreek aids digestion and can prevent wind and helps relieve flatulence and diarrhoea.

• It used to be said that fenugreek cured baldness in men, and it's still used in Indonesia as a hair tonic.

garlic

Garlic is one of the most popular and widely used flavourings in the world. Its sharp, punchy taste and pungent smell make it indispensable in any kitchen, and it understandably plays a major part in a vast number of the world's finest dishes.

For centuries garlic has been renowned, for both great culinary and medicinal powers. It is the bulb of a plant related to the onion family, native to Asia but today grown in warm countries all over the world. There are many different varieties – white, pink and mauve – the most common being the white, papery-skinned variety. The bulbs vary in size and in their flavour, which can range from mild and sweet to sharp, pungent and very strong. A good bulb of garlic should be firm and tightly packed, and the cloves should be moist, not shrivelled or too dry. The powerful aroma of garlic is released when the garlic is peeled and chopped or crushed. The best way to chop garlic is to peel and roughly chop it on a board, then crush with the flat side of a sharp knife or use a pestle and mortar. Raw garlic is incredibly strong, but when cooked, the flavour mellows and becomes much milder – garlic roasted in its skin has a wonderful mellow, sweet, nutty flavour. If you want only a faint hint of garlic, just rub the cut side of a clove on the cooking vessel or on the food you want to flavour. Dried garlic is also available; you can buy garlic salt and granules, which in some cases can be substituted for fresh garlic. Try not to allow the garlic to brown when frying, as this will give it a bitter taste. To freshen your breath after eating garlic, try chewing fresh parsley or fennel seeds.

Culinary uses

It's difficult to imagine cooking without garlic when preparing casseroles, stews, soups and pasta sauces, meat, poultry, game, fish, vegetables, salads, dips, pizzas and many more dishes – just think of the wondrous garlic sauces of the Mediterranean such as aïoli and rouille.

• Cut garlic into slivers and insert into meat, or add to pasta sauce.

• For a hint of garlic in a salad, rub the inside of the salad bowl with the side of a cut clove of garlic, before adding the salad.

• Dried garlic can often be used in place of fresh garlic – try adding a few dried garlic granules to Yorkshire pudding batter, or sprinkle them into salad dressings and mayonnaise.

• Marinade olives in olive oil, garlic granules and oregano.

• For a dip, add chopped onion and garlic to soured cream and chives.

• A leg of lamb rubbed with some garlic granules, salt and rosemary just before roasting is especially delicious.

• Add garlic salt and olive oil to cooked and drained green beans.

• Garlic bread is the UK's most popular restaurant starter. To make it yourself, slice a loaf of French bread diagonally at 2cm (¾in) intervals. Spread each slice with softened butter and sprinkle with Garlic Bread Seasoning. Reshape the bread, wrap it well in foil and bake in a preheated moderate oven for 10–15 minutes.

Did you know...?

• Garlic can help to prevent blood clots forming.

• In addition, it helps lower blood pressure, can help regulate cholesterol levels and is said to boost the immune system.

• Some herbalists also claim that garlic aids digestion and can help to prevent flatulence.

Serves 4
Preparation 20 mins
Cooking 20 mins
Calories 509
Fat 16g

350g (12oz) dried spaghetti
1kg (2lb 4oz) fresh mussels
2 tbsp olive oil, plus 1 tbsp
extra for drizzling
2 shallots, finely chopped
4 garlic cloves, chopped
150ml (¼ pint) dry white wine
Grated rind of ½ lemon
½ tsp dried chilli flakes
2 tbsp chopped fresh parsley
Black pepper

Chilli-spiked mussels with spaghetti

1 Cook the pasta according to packet instructions.
Meanwhile, scrub the mussels under cold running
water, and discard any that are open or damaged.
Place in a large heavy-based saucepan, with just
the water clinging to the shells. Steam for 3–4
minutes over a high heat, shaking regularly, until the
shells have opened. Discard any closed mussels.

2 Heat 2 tablespoons of oil in a large saucepan
and gently fry the shallots and garlic for 5 minutes
until softened. Add the wine and boil for 5–6
minutes to reduce by half. Add the mussels, lemon
rind and chilli. Heat for 2–3 minutes. Add the pasta,
then stir in the parsley and black pepper. Toss over
a gentle heat and drizzle over the remaining oil.

39

Serves 4

Preparation 20 mins

Cooking 12 mins

Calories 398

Fat 11g

250g pack dried fine
egg noodles
2 tbsp groundnut oil
2 skinless boneless chicken
breasts, cut into strips
2 tbsp oyster sauce
3 tbsp dark soy sauce
1 yellow pepper, deseeded
and chopped
1cm (½in) piece fresh root
ginger, finely chopped
1 garlic clove, finely chopped
2 tbsp Schwartz Thai
Lemongrass and Coconut
Stir-fry Seasoning (optional)
170g pack mangetout
2 spring onions,
sliced diagonally
Fresh coriander and 1 red
chilli, deseeded and sliced,
to garnish

Stir-fry noodles & chicken

1 Cook the noodles in boiling water according to
packet instructions. Drain, rinse and set aside.

2 Heat a wok, then, when hot, add the oil. Stir-fry
the chicken for 2 minutes with half the oyster sauce
and soy sauce. Add the pepper, ginger, garlic and
seasoning, if using, and fry for a further 3 minutes.

3 Add the mangetout and spring onions to the
chicken and stir-fry for another minute. Add the
noodles, mixing well, then stir in the remaining soy
and oyster sauces. Stir-fry for 4 minutes, until the
noodles are heated through. Garnish with the
coriander and chilli.

ginger

The warm, sweet, tangy flavour of ginger is in a class of its own and it is an essential ingredient in both Western and Eastern cookery – from traditional ginger biscuits and breads to Indian and South-East Asian curries and Chinese stir-fries.

Ginger is the underground stem or rhizome of an iris-like plant grown widely in the tropics. Fresh ginger has thick, papery skin but it's equally good in powder form – 1 teaspoon of ground ginger is equivalent to a 2.5cm (1in) piece of fresh root ginger. The taste of ginger is quite hot and spicy, but with an underlying warmth that really livens up the palate.

Culinary uses

Ginger provides the heart and soul of a huge number and wide variety of sweet and savoury dishes. It is used in breads, biscuits, cakes, curries, stews and stir-fries, as well as wines and cordials.

- It is frequently included in Indian curry powders, while in Morocco it is used to flavour couscous and almond and honey desserts.
- Marinade fish with ginger, sherry and garlic before cooking.
- Use finely shredded ginger in stir-fry dishes to add a spicy warmth.

Did you know...?

- Ginger is said to improve poor circulation, promote sweating and alleviate colds.

- A teaspoon of ginger in warm water helps prevent sickness of all kinds, especially travel sickness and morning sickness.

juniper berries

*The bitter-sweet taste of the juniper berry is best known as
a flavouring for gin, but in marinades and pickles, and in sweet
and savoury dishes, they give a distinctly pleasant, sweet taste.
They add heartiness to rich beef and game stews and roasts.*

Juniper berries are the deep purple fruit of the juniper bush, which
grows across the northern hemisphere. The further south they grow,
the more flavour they have. When dried, they become more purply-black
in colour. The taste is bitter-sweet, quite resiny and with a peppery
aftertaste. Lightly crush the berries before use to release their flavour.

Culinary uses

Although best with sweet dishes, juniper berries can also be used to
flavour rich beef stews, pork and venison, and terrines. Juniper is used
in the mountainous regions of Italy, France and Germany to flavour rich
game dishes. Sauerkraut is traditionally flavoured with juniper berries.

• Adding a few crushed juniper berries to a conventional stuffing for
roast chicken can give sublime results.

• Crushed juniper berries make a tasty spiced vodka. Add 10 lightly
crushed juniper berries and 3–5 small chillies to a bottle of good-quality
vodka, then leave for 2–3 weeks before drinking.

• Add a little crushed juniper to rich fruit cakes such as Christmas
cake, and Christmas pudding, for added pungency.

• Juniper berries go especially well with apples and other stewed fruits.
Try adding crushed juniper berries to apple crumble or a fruit tart.

lemongrass

If you are a fan of Thai, Malaysian and Indonesian food, you will be familiar with the distinctive, bright, lemony flavour and highly perfumed scent of lemongrass, which is a key feature of many South-East Asian dishes, from soups to stir-fries.

Lemongrass is a tropical grass that comes from South-East Asia, where its perfumed lemony flavour adds a distinctive note to local dishes. Fresh lemongrass stems are tough; the root can be crushed or finely sliced, before using, or the stem can be used whole, then removed before serving. Alternatively, use dried lemongrass – 1 teaspoon of dried lemongrass is equivalent to one fresh stalk. Dried lemongrass is best soaked in a little water for a couple of hours before using.

Culinary uses

Lemongrass is used mainly in South-East Asian cooking, in soups, stir-fries, fish cakes, rice dishes and various curries.

• Hot and sour soup from South-East Asia is made with a good fish stock, chillies and lemongrass, with added prawns and spring onions.

• Lemongrass is a perfect partner for coconut milk, especially in dishes with chicken, fish or seafood.

• For Oriental steamed fish, mix together lemongrass, ginger, chillies and shallots with a little soy sauce and rice wine. Cut slits in the fish, pour over the sauce and marinate before steaming.

• For chicken satay, marinate chicken pieces in lemongrass, ginger, garlic, crushed chillies and a little oil, then thread on skewers and grill.

43

Serves 2

Preparation 15 mins

Cooking 30 mins

Calories 757

Fat 36g

400g can chopped tomatoes

2 tbsp olive oil

250g (9oz) mushrooms,

wiped and thinly sliced

2 small garlic cloves,

peeled and finely chopped

Salt and black pepper

1 tsp dried marjoram

2 x 25cm (10in) pizza bases

2 tbsp finely grated

Parmesan

150g (5oz) mozzarella,

roughly chopped

Mushroom pizza

1 Put the tomatoes in a saucepan and cook over a medium heat for 15–20 minutes, stirring from time to time, until the sauce has reduced and thickened.

2 Meanwhile, preheat the oven to the highest setting – usually 240°C/475°F/Gas Mark 9. Heat the oil in a frying pan over a medium heat for 1 minute. Sauté the mushrooms, garlic, salt, pepper and marjoram for 7–10 minutes, until tender.

3 Place the pizza bases on a baking tray. Divide the tomato sauce between each base and spread to the edges with a spoon. Scatter half of the cooked mushroom mixture evenly over each pizza. Sprinkle with Parmesan and mozzarella. Bake for 8–10 minutes, until the topping is golden and bubbling.

marjoram

This delicately perfumed herb, closely related to thyme and oregano, is a hugely important culinary herb, whose uses are many and varied, fresh or dried. Marjoram brings that sweet, heady scent of the Mediterranean to your kitchen.

You can buy sweet or pot marjoram, both of which come from the Mediterranean. Sweet marjoram, as its name suggests, is sweeter than the pot variety and has a slightly more delicate taste. Marjoram is similar in some ways to thyme and can be added to almost any dish that would normally include it. Marjoram has an enormous number and range of uses, but it is perhaps best known as one of the ingredients in traditional mixed herbs along with sage and thyme. To preserve its delicate perfume, marjoram is best added moments before the end of cooking. It can be used raw in salad dressings and marinades as well.

Culinary uses

Marjoram adds marvellous flavour to lamb, chicken, veal, pork and fish, vegetables, cheese and eggs. It is traditionally used in tomato sauces and is widely found in Italian and Mexican dishes.

• Marinate and baste lamb or chicken with a dressing of olive oil, lemon juice, salt and marjoram. Grill or barbecue and serve with wedges of lemon. A similar dressing, perhaps with the addition of crushed chillies, can be used with fresh sardines, before grilling.

• Sprinkle raw fresh marjoram on to salads or grilled vegetables.

• Marjoram can also be infused in milk and added to milk puddings.

45

mint

New potatoes, fresh peas and roast lamb wouldn't be half as good without the addition of this popular herb. Mint is synonymous with summer because of its refreshing taste and sweet aroma that is appealing to almost everyone.

Although mint was introduced to Britain by the Romans, its use as a flavouring in many countries dates back to antiquity. In India it is associated with chutneys and pickles, in Britain with lamb and mint sauce and in the Middle East with minced lamb. Wherever it is used, mint, with its refreshing flavour and clean, distinct aroma, always adds an extra dimension to both sweet and savoury dishes. There are now many different varieties of mint, mostly native to the Mediterranean. The leaves are usually small and bright green, although some varieties are variegated and others have larger leaves. Dried mint has a more subtle aroma and taste. The most commonly used mint in cooking is spearmint, also known as common or garden mint. The varieties pineapple mint, large-leafed Bowles mint, and peppermint are also used for culinary purposes. Mint doesn't mix well with other herbs or other strong flavours because it is such a powerful flavouring itself.

Did you know...?

- Peppermint and spearmint are the varieties most commonly used for medicinal purposes.

- Mint is often used in cold remedies and throat lozenges.
- Drinking peppermint tea is said to aid digestion.

Summer Tabbouleh

Serves 4

Preparation 25 mins

Cooking 10 mins

Calories 220

Fat 15g

175g (6oz) bulgar wheat
2 medium eggs
1 red onion, finely chopped
2 garlic cloves, finely chopped
1 red and 1 yellow pepper,
cored, deseeded and
finely chopped
1 tbsp each chopped fresh
parsley, chives and coriander
3 tbsp chopped fresh mint
Grated rind and
juice of 1 lemon
Grated rind and
juice of 1 lime
3 tbsp olive oil
Salt and black pepper

1 Prepare the bulgar wheat according to packet instructions. Meanwhile, bring a saucepan of water to the boil. Add the eggs and boil for 10 minutes. Cool under cold running water, then remove the shells and mash the eggs.

2 Add the onion, garlic, peppers, parsley, chives, coriander, mint, lemon and lime rind and juice, and the oil to the bulgar wheat, then mix well. Season to taste before serving.

Culinary uses

Mint is much used in Middle Eastern, Indian and Greek cookery; it is traditionally chosen in Britain as a summer herb for flavouring lamb, new potatoes and peas. With lamb, veal, rabbit, fish and tomatoes, in salads, soups, jelly, ice cream and fresh fruits, it is truly wonderful.

• It's used in many Middle Eastern dishes such as tabbouleh, a salad made with bulgar wheat, tomatoes, mint, parsley and lemon juice.

• In India, mint makes raitas – cooling side dishes for hot curries.

• It is also added to many Indian chutneys and pickles.

• To make mint sauce for roast lamb, place a dessertspoon of dried mint in a jug with a little hot water and sugar and vinegar to taste.

• Mint tea is very refreshing in summer and is said to aid the digestion. In India mint tea is preferred milky, while the Arabs enjoy a more refreshing infusion of hot water, fresh mint and plenty of sugar. You can also try mixing a few dried mint leaves with packet tea.

• Mint makes a delightful addition to a number of summer drinks. Infused in cordials and fresh fruit juices, it is very cooling on a hot summer's day, and it is a traditional ingredient of the classic British summer cocktail – Pimms No 1.

• Make your own Greek dish of dolmades (stuffed vine leaves) by stuffing vine leaves or cabbage leaves with a mixture of rice, minced lamb, tomatoes, onion, parsley and mint, then steam them over a pan of boiling water until cooked through.

• Sprinkle 1–2 teaspoons of dried mint on tomato halves, then drizzle with olive oil before grilling, frying or roasting them.

• Although rarely paired, mint with fish works well: include mint in fillings for fish, or in a simple lemon dressing to drizzle over grilled fish.

• Tear a few leaves over fresh fruit salads to add colour and flavour.

Serves 4–6

Preparation 20 mins

plus 30 mins standing

Cooking 45 mins

Calories 424

Fat 15g

40g (1½oz) sunflower spread,
plus extra for greasing
6 medium slices
wholemeal bread
125g (4oz) sultanas
Finely grated rind
of 1 small lemon
40g (1½oz) soft light
brown sugar
½ tsp each ground nutmeg
and ground mace
2 medium eggs
600ml (1 pint) half-fat milk

Lemony bread pudding

1 Grease a 23 x 28cm (9 x 11in) ovenproof dish.
Spread one side of each bread slice with sunflower
spread, then cut each one into four triangles and
arrange half of them in the dish, spread-side up.

2 Mix together the sultanas, lemon rind, half the
sugar and half the spices, then sprinkle over the
bread. Arrange the remaining bread over the top,
spread-side up, and sprinkle with the remaining
sugar and spices.

3 Beat together the eggs and milk and pour over
the bread. Set aside for 30 minutes to allow the
bread to absorb some of the liquid. Preheat the
oven to 180°C/350°F/Gas Mark 4. Bake for
45 minutes, until lightly set and golden brown.

nutmeg & mace

These closely related spices that come from the fruit of the same plant have a similar rich, warm, sweet, nutty flavour and perfumed sweet aroma that go particularly well with milk and cheese dishes, either sweet or savoury.

Nutmeg is the oval seed, with a dusty brown coat; inside it is lighter brown and patterned. Mace is the scarlet lacy covering. When dried, mace is yellowy-red. They both have a rich, warm, aromatic flavour, but nutmeg is slightly sweeter. Mace has a more delicate taste and is used mainly in savoury dishes such as clear soups and sauces. Nutmeg can be used in both sweet and savoury dishes.

Culinary uses

Nutmeg and mace add a sweetness and warmth to beef, seafood, veal, vegetables, potatoes, and tomato and white sauces.

- Add a pinch of nutmeg to béchamel sauce or mashed potato.
- Add nutmeg to Italian pasta dishes such as Bolognese sauce or stuffings for tortellini, ravioli and cannelloni.
- Try sprinkling freshly grated nutmeg on to spinach soup.

Did you know...?

- Nutmeg can help to ease digestive disorders and some people say it relieves insomnia.

- In some countries nutmeg is considered to be an aphrodisiac, but if eaten in large quantities it can cause hallucinations.

oregano

The Mediterranean kitchen just wouldn't be the same without the sweet pervading perfume of oregano. Its robust flavour is the essence of so many wonderful southern European dishes, particularly those with tomatoes, aubergines and beans.

Also known as wild marjoram because it belongs to the same family, oregano could be substituted for marjoram in most recipes. However, oregano is stronger, spicier and more robust-tasting than marjoram and retains its flavour better, even over long periods of cooking, thanks to its high concentration of essential oils.

Culinary uses

Lamb, chicken, veal, pork, fish, stuffings, eggs, tomatoes, vegetables, cheese, pizza and most other Italian foods all benefit from the addition of oregano. It's known as the 'pizza herb' because it's traditionally used to flavour pizza toppings, as well as many other Mediterranean dishes. It goes especially well with tomatoes, peppers and aubergines.

• Use oregano in tomato-based pasta sauces.

• Add a generous sprinkling of chopped fresh or dried oregano to stuffings for fish or vegetables, which can then be roasted or grilled.

• Flavour oils and vinegars with a few sprigs of oregano.

• Oregano is excellent with vegetables – sauté sliced courgettes in oil, butter, garlic and a sprinkling of oregano.

• Rub dried oregano leaves on top of halved tomatoes or thinly sliced aubergines, brushed with olive oil, before grilling or roasting them.

Serves 4

Preparation 15 mins

Cooking 30 mins

Calories 612

Fat 26g

100ml (4fl oz) extra
virgin olive oil
2 garlic cloves, finely sliced
1 aubergine, peeled and cubed
1 red pepper and 1 yellow
pepper, deseeded and cubed
400g can chopped tomatoes
100ml (4fl oz) dry white wine
Salt and black pepper
375g (13oz) dried pasta
spirals (stortelli)
2 tbsp chopped
fresh oregano
12 black olives, pitted
and sliced, to garnish

Stortelli & sweet peppers

1 Heat 5 tablespoons of the oil in a large heavy-based saucepan. Fry the garlic for 1 minute to release its flavour. Add the aubergine and peppers and cook, uncovered, stirring frequently, for about 5 minutes, or until just browned.

2 Add the tomatoes, boil for 5 minutes to reduce the liquid slightly, then add the wine. Bring back to the boil and season. Cook, partly covered, for 20 minutes until the vegetables are tender.

3 Meanwhile, cook the pasta according to packet instructions until al dente. Transfer to a warmed serving bowl and toss with the remaining oil and half the sauce. Spoon over the remaining sauce and garnish with the oregano and olives.

Serves 4

Preparation 15 mins

Cooking 1 hr

Calories 443

Fat 31g

8 chicken joints, such as
thighs and drumsticks

2 tbsp olive oil

1 onion, sliced

2 garlic cloves, crushed

1 red and 1 yellow pepper,
deseeded and sliced

2 tsp paprika

50ml (2fl oz) dry sherry
or dry vermouth

400g can chopped tomatoes

1 bay leaf

1 strip orange rind, pared
with a vegetable peeler

70g (2½oz) chorizo, sliced

50g (2oz) pitted black olives

Salt and black pepper

Spanish chicken & chorizo

1 Place the chicken in a large non-stick frying pan
and fry without oil for 5–8 minutes, turning
occasionally, until golden. Remove the chicken and
set aside, then pour away any fat from the pan.

2 Add the olive oil to the pan and fry the onion,
garlic and peppers for 3–4 minutes, until softened.
Return the chicken to the pan with the paprika,
sherry, tomatoes, bay leaf and orange rind. Bring to
the boil, cover the pan, then simmer over a low heat
for 35–40 minutes, stirring occasionally, until the
chicken is cooked through.

3 Add the chorizo and olives and simmer for a
further 5 minutes to heat through, then season.

paprika

This deep red peppery powder with its mild flavour and striking colour is perhaps best known as the flavouring for Hungarian goulash, but it is also widely used in many hearty Spanish dishes, spicy sausages and fish dishes.

Paprika is a deep red, slightly earthy-flavoured ground spice that comes from the dried sweet red pepper of the capsicum family from which the seeds and inner membranes have been removed. It's closely related to the hot chilli pepper, but doesn't have the same heat; it's much more mild, with a sweet, lightly pungent flavour and slightly bitter aftertaste. Buy it in small amounts and use fairly quickly as the flavour can deteriorate quickly. Good paprika should be bright red; the older it is, the duller the colour becomes. You can buy hot or mild paprika – the hottest can be comparable to chilli powder, so always check the label.

Culinary uses

Paprika complements pork, chicken, veal, vegetables, cheese and egg dishes. It's the national spice of Hungary and gives Hungarian goulash – a warming winter stew – its characteristic flavour and taste.

- Use a healthy sprinkling of paprika in chicken casseroles.
- Paprika makes a colourful garnish if sprinkled on to mayonnaise, béchamel and white sauces and creamy soups.
- Give Swiss rösti an appetising colour by tossing the raw grated potato in a little paprika before frying.
- Add paprika to fish stews to add warmth and heartiness.

parsley

With its deep green frilled or larger, flatter leaves, parsley is one of the best known and most widely used herbs the world over, both for garnishing and in cooking. It's as popular in the street bazaars of the Middle East as in French 'haute cuisine'.

Parsley is so adaptable that it's little wonder it appears in so many recipes all over the world, from the old cockney favourite 'Liquor', a green sauce served with pie and mash, to the more exotic Middle Eastern dishes, such as *Fattoush*, a Lebanese salad, and the Moroccan tabbouleh salad. You can buy both flatleaf and curly-leaved parsley these days; the curly-leaved is the more traditional variety but flatleaf parsley is said to have more flavour and is more prominent in Italian cookery. The stalks contain much of the flavour so shouldn't be left out – use them in stocks and sauces or include them in a bouquet garni. Because its flavour isn't overpowering, parsley blends very well with other herbs and can be used liberally in a multitude of dishes.

Culinary uses

A sprig of curly-leaved parsley provides an attractive finishing touch to a wide variety of savoury dishes and its mild taste is perfect with fish. Parsley is a good accompaniment to lamb, chicken, ham, vegetables, egg and cheese dishes, soups and sauces. Try deep-frying parsley and serving it as a side vegetable, or use it fresh in green salads.

• Parsley is an essential ingredient in a bouquet garni and in the French combination of *fines herbes*, used for many grills and fish dishes.

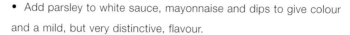

- It's also good with basil and mint in *Fattoush,* the Lebanese salad.

- Add parsley to white sauce, mayonnaise and dips to give colour and a mild, but very distinctive, flavour.

- To make parsley sauce, simply heat some milk with the stalks of a bunch of parsley. Bring to a simmer, then take off the heat. Chop the leaves finely. Strain the milk, remove the stalks and stir in the chopped leaves. Add cream and more parsley to taste. It's delectable with ham, broad beans, mashed potato or smoked fish, such as trout or haddock.

- Toss a tablespoon or more of parsley into all types of salads including potato, pasta, lentil and green salads. It's nice to keep the leaves whole or in small sprigs so they add texture as well as flavour.

- Parsley is an excellent garnish for white fish such as cod, plaice or sole as it doesn't overpower the delicate flavour of the fish.

- To make garlic mushrooms, sauté mushrooms in butter, chopped garlic and a generous tablespoon of chopped parsley. This is very good with *chanterelles* – a French mushroom variety with a lovely winy flavour.

- For garlic and parsley prawns, heat some butter and oil in a frying pan, add garlic, onion, parsley and prawns and stir-fry until sizzling.

- Make parsley butter by creaming butter with garlic, parsley, lemon juice, salt and pepper. Chill for 30 minutes and serve with grilled food.

Did you know...?

- Parsley contains vitamin C and potassium and surprisingly high levels of iron.
- Due to its high content of chlorophyll, parsley is a very good deodorant! Chewing a sprig of parsley freshens the breath, and if you've been chopping garlic, rub your fingers in some chopped parsley afterwards to help remove any lingering smell.

Serves 4

Preparation 20 mins

Cooking 1 hr 45 mins

Calories 397

Fat 21g

1 tbsp olive or sunflower oil

1 large onion, chopped

1 large carrot, finely chopped

50g (2oz) bacon, chopped

750g (1lb 11oz) beef
steak mince

300ml (½ pint) beef stock

2 tbsp tomato ketchup

1 tbsp Worcestershire sauce

1 tsp chopped fresh thyme

Salt and black pepper

2 tbsp chopped fresh
parsley, plus extra,
to garnish

900g (2lb) potato,
cooked and mashed

400g (14oz) swede,
cooked and mashed

25g (1oz) butter

Cottage (or Clapshot) pie

1 Heat the oil in a frying pan, then fry the onion,
carrot and bacon for 10 minutes, until browned.
Add the mince and fry for 10–15 minutes, breaking
up any lumps, until the meat has browned.

2 Spoon off excess fat. Add the stock, ketchup,
Worcestershire sauce, thyme and season. Simmer,
partly covered, for 45 minutes, stirring from time to
time, until thickened. Add a little water, if necessary.

3 Preheat the oven to 200°C/400°F/Gas Mark 6.
Transfer the beef to a 1.5 litre (2¾ pint) shallow
ovenproof dish, then stir in the parsley. Mix together
the potato and swede, smooth over the pie and dot
with the butter. Bake for 35–40 minutes, until
browned. Garnish with parsley.

59

Serves 4

Preparation 10 mins

Cooking 10 mins

Calories 340

Fat 15g

4 thick fillet steaks, about
160g (5½oz) each
2 tbsp olive oil
3 tbsp mixed whole
peppercorns, crushed
400ml (14fl oz) red wine
200ml (7fl oz) stock, made
with ¼ beef-stock cube
Salt

Steak au poivre

1 Brush the steaks with 1 tablespoon of the olive
oil, then press the peppercorns well in around the
edge of each steak with your fingers.

2 Heat the remaining oil in a large heavy-based
frying pan over a medium to high heat. Cook the
steaks for 5–6 minutes, turning once, until cooked.
(Cooking times will vary depending on the thickness
of the steaks, so check that they are cooked to your
liking before removing from the pan.)

3 Transfer the steaks to serving plates and keep
warm. Lower the heat, then add the wine and stock
to the pan. Boil for 4–5 minutes or until reduced by
half. Add salt to taste and spoon the sauce over
the steaks to serve.

pepper

Known as the 'king of spices', pepper is undoubtedly the oldest and most widely used spice in the world. Once it was so highly valued that it was literally worth its weight in gold. You can add pepper to absolutely any savoury dish you can think of.

Peppercorns are the berries of a tropical vine that originated in the south-west of India. It has a warm, pungent flavour and a hot, biting taste. Not only important as a seasoning, it also enhances the flavour of many foods – try freshly ground black pepper with fresh strawberries or melon and you'll be amazed at the result. Black peppercorns come from the green unripe berries, which are dried and become black and shrivelled in the sun. White pepper is the same fruit with the dark outer husk removed. Both are available whole or ground. Their warm, pungent flavour is released on grinding and is enhanced by heat. After grinding, the volatile oils soon evaporate, so add freshly ground black or white pepper at the table or towards the end of cooking.

Culinary uses

Pepper can be used in all savoury dishes. Add freshly ground pepper to stocks, pickles and marinades, and drop a few whole peppercorns into soups, stews and casseroles.

- Coarsely ground black pepper in an olive oil dressing enhances wafer-thin slices of marinated meat, or fish such as smoked salmon.
- Try the culinary classic steak au poivre or, alternatively, tuna au poivre.
- Add white pepper to white sauces and béchamel sauce.

rosemary

A powerful and potent herb, rosemary is traditionally used with lamb and chicken in Mediterranean dishes. But this versatile and distinctive herb can enliven pork, fish and potatoes. It's especially good with anything cooked on the barbecue.

Rosemary is the hard, needle-shaped leaf of a small evergreen shrub that grows wild in profusion in the Mediterranean. It has a potent pine-wood aroma and a powerful, bittersweet flavour. You only have to crush the leaves between your fingers for the aroma to become quite assertive. Because it is so powerful, rosemary is best used in moderation. When cooking with rosemary, add a whole sprig to the dish, but remove it just before serving, as the leaves are quite tough. Rosemary dries well, too.

Culinary uses

Although rosemary is the traditional partner to roast lamb, it also marries well with other meats such as pork, chicken and game. It will enhance oily fish, vegetables, tomato sauce, soups and marinades. And it can be used in sweet dishes, infused in creams, custards and sauces.

- Tuck sprigs of rosemary into joints of meat before roasting.
- Rosemary with olive oil, garlic and lemon juice is a fresh and lively marinade for meats and oily fish.
- For duck and other game, serve a rich red wine and rosemary gravy.
- Roast, grill or fry potatoes with rosemary.
- Add the herb to barbecue coals for an aromatic smoky flavour.
- You can also add dried rosemary to a scone mixture and fruit salads.

Serves 4
Preparation 5 mins
Cooking 40 mins
Calories 88
Fat 6g

600g (1lb 5oz) shallots
or pickling onions
2 tbsp olive oil
1–2 tbsp chopped
fresh rosemary
Black pepper

Roasted shallots with rosemary

1 Preheat the oven to 200°C/400°F/Gas Mark 6. Place the shallots in a roasting tin, drizzle over the oil, sprinkle with the rosemary and black pepper, then toss to mix well.

2 Cook in the oven for 30–40 minutes, basting once or twice during cooking, until the shallots are tender and golden brown. Serve hot.

saffron

Saffron is the world's most expensive and, in many countries, most highly prized spice. Rice – in pilaus, paellas, risottos – is the best partner for saffron, but it is also heavenly in buns, cakes and creamy puddings, and with chicken and fish.

Saffron is the dried, red stigmas of the autumn-flowering crocus. It's known as much for its properties as a dye as for its unique bitter sweet, honey-like flavour and pungent aroma. Saffron is cultivated in many Mediterranean countries and it used to be grown in England, in Saffron Walden, until the turn of the century. Hence the old English recipes incorporating saffron, such as Saffron buns. Today, however, Spanish saffron from La Mancha is considered to be the best. The saffron stigmas are fine, bright, orange-red ragged threads, about 2.5cm (1in) long; the deeper the colour the better the quality. You can buy saffron ready-ground, although it may be adulterated. Just a little saffron gives food a glorious rich gold colour. For an even flavour and colour, steep a pinch of crushed saffron strands in a little hot water before adding both the liquid and saffron to the dish. Use it sparingly.

Culinary uses

Saffron lends colour and flavour to the rice dishes paella, pilau and risotto, to chicken, fish, curries, potatoes, buns, yogurt and cream.

- Add crushed saffron strands directly to the water when cooking rice.
- It's used in bouillabaisse, the delicious French fish stew.
- Saffron is also an essential ingredient in rouille, served with fish soup.

Serves 4

Preparation 10 mins

Cooking 25 mins

Calories 240

Fat 6g

1 tbsp olive oil

Salt and black pepper

12 thin-cut pork loin steaks

300ml (½ pint) chicken stock

Finely grated rind and
juice of 1 orange

2 tbsp dry sherry or
dry vermouth

2 tbsp redcurrant jelly

2 tsp chopped fresh sage
or 1 tsp dried sage

Steamed shredded cabbage,
to serve

Pan-fried pork with orange

1 Heat the oil in a large heavy-based frying pan.
Season the steaks well with salt and black pepper,
add 6 steaks to the pan and fry for 4 minutes on
each side or until cooked. Remove from the pan
and keep warm while you fry the remaining steaks.
Add them to the first batch and keep warm.

2 Add the stock, orange rind and juice, sherry
or vermouth and redcurrant jelly to the pan. Cook
vigorously over a high heat for 5 minutes, stirring,
or until reduced by half and darkened in colour.

3 Stir the sage into the sauce and season to taste.
Return the steaks to the pan and warm through for
1–2 minutes. Serve on a bed of shredded cabbage
and spoon the sauce over.

sage

Sunday roast would be a pale shadow of itself without sage and onion stuffing. Sage is at its best with fatty meats like pork and duck, but this strongly aromatic herb is also good in cheese and egg dishes or with tomatoes and garlic.

There are several different varieties of sage, but the most popular for cooking is the purple-flowering, grey-leaved sage. Its soft, velvety leaves have a wonderful, heady scent and powerful flavour, but use them sparingly. It's a favourite culinary herb that can withstand long cooking.

Culinary uses

Sage has a particular affinity with onions, tomatoes and garlic. It also goes well with pork, duck, veal, game, poultry, sausages and stuffings, vegetables, salads, cheese and eggs.

- In Italy sage is dipped into a light batter, then deep-fried and served as an appetiser. Or it's sprinkled on to salads, pasta and gnocchi.
- Combine a little sage with cheese and breadcrumbs for topping grilled fish or as a stuffing for meats.
- Use sage to give minestrone soup extra flavour.

Did you know...?

- Used as a mouthwash, sage is said to freshen the breath and helps to prevent bleeding gums.

- Traditionally, a sage bath was used to relieve rheumatism and fight fatigue. Sage tea was also used to help soothe sore throats.

---

tarragon

This aromatic herb is one of the great culinary herbs used widely in French cooking. Its distinctive tart flavour has a real affinity with chicken and eggs, and it is a key ingredient of classic sauces such as hollandaise and tartare sauce.

The long, slim, green leaves of tarragon have a strong, spicy, aniseed flavour, and a cooling quality; they are also intensely aromatic, especially when crushed. There are two main types of tarragon – French and Russian – but the French variety is far superior and is the only one recommended for cooking. Russian tarragon has a duller, earthy taste. Use tarragon with caution, however, as it can overpower other ingredients and take on a bitter taste.

Culinary uses

Tarragon is particularly used in dishes of French origin, has an affinity with chicken (as in the classic French dish *poulet à l'estragon*), and complements veal, lamb, fish, eggs, salads, sauces, vegetables, soups and mayonnaise. Tarragon is also used to flavour classic French sauces such as béarnaise, hollandaise and tartare, and for flavouring vinegars for salad dressings and sauces.

• Tarragon is superb in salads, with fish, and with egg dishes such as omelettes and eggs baked in cream.

• Remoulade sauce made with mayonnaise, mustard, chopped capers, gherkins and tarragon is excellent served with fish, meat or vegetables.

• Add tarragon to wine vinegar, to flavour it, and use for a vinaigrette.

Serves 4

Preparation 5 mins

Cooking 40 mins

Calories 456

Fat 28g

600ml (1 pint) chicken stock
200ml (7fl oz) dry white wine
1 sprig fresh tarragon,
plus extra to garnish
200ml (7fl oz) double cream
1 tbsp olive oil
Salt and black pepper
4 turkey breast steaks,
about 175g (6oz) each,
halved lengthways
2 tsp Dijon mustard
1 tsp lemon juice,
or to taste

Turkey & tarragon sauce

1 Place the stock and wine in a small saucepan and bring to the boil. Add the tarragon and simmer for about 15 minutes to reduce the liquid by half. Pour in the cream and simmer for 10–15 minutes more, until the sauce is reduced by a further third. Discard the tarragon.

2 Meanwhile, heat the oil in a large frying pan, season the turkey and fry for 4–5 minutes on both sides, until golden and cooked through.

3 Add the mustard and lemon juice to the sauce, then add the sauce to the turkey. Scrape the bottom of the frying pan with a wooden spatula to mix the pan juices with the sauce. Serve the turkey and sauce garnished with tarragon leaves.

Serves 6

Preparation 20 mins

Cooking 1 hr 30 mins

Calories 709

Fat 45g

1 tbsp olive oil
6 rashers rindless
streaky bacon, cut into
2.5cm (1in) pieces
1 large onion, roughly sliced
200g (7oz) carrots, chopped
3 tbsp chopped fresh thyme,
or 2 tsp dried thyme
Salt and black pepper
4 x 300g cans flageolet
beans, drained
2 x 454g packs sausages,
cut into 2.5cm (1in) slices
300ml (½ pint) chicken or
vegetable stock

Winter sausage casserole

1 Preheat the oven to 200°C/400°F/Gas Mark 6.
Heat the oil in a large heavy-based frying pan. Add
the bacon and fry for 3–4 minutes, until the fat has
browned. Add the onion and carrots and fry for
6–8 minutes, until they start to colour.

2 Place half the bacon mixture in an ovenproof
casserole dish, sprinkle with half the thyme, and
season. Top with half the beans and sausages,
then repeat the layers.

3 Pour the stock into the casserole, cover and
cook in the oven for 1 hour. Increase the heat to
230°C/450°F/Gas Mark 8. Remove the lid and cook
for a further 10–15 minutes, until browned. Serve
piping hot, straight from the oven.

thyme

This well-loved and incredibly versatile herb is an essential part of a bouquet garni. Thyme can be used in stuffings for chicken and pork, and many casseroles and pasta sauces would not taste as good without its intensely aromatic presence.

Thyme is undoubtedly one of the most useful culinary herbs. It can withstand long cooking without losing its highly perfumed flavour, so it is an ideal choice for many slow-cooked casseroles and stews. It lends a pungent, distinctive taste to many dishes, so is often used in recipes that require strong flavourings, such as sausages, pâtés and pickles. There are around 100 different varieties of thyme, both wild and cultivated, but 'common' thyme is the one most often used in cooking. The tiny oval, grey-green leaves contain robust essential oils and are deliciously aromatic. You can also find flavoured thymes such as caraway, lemon and orange thyme, the latter two are both good with fish dishes. Despite its distinctive flavour and strength of character, thyme is not an overpowering herb, so it can be used in innumerable dishes and it combines well with other herbs such as marjoram and sage. It is one of the essential herbs (along with parsley, marjoram and bay) included in the classic bouquet garni, where it lends a deep, rich flavour to many casseroles, soups, stocks and marinades. Good-quality dried thyme should contain very little twig or stalk and should retain its grey-green colour. The easiest way to use thyme is to strip the leaves off the stalk – if you strip the leaves downwards from the top end, they should come off very easily, leaving the woody stalk behind.

Culinary uses

Thyme is such a lovely, versatile herb that it can be used in numerous different ways: for example, it combines well with chicken, lamb, beef, offal, rabbit and turkey equally as well as with vegetables, fish, cheese and eggs. Thyme's aromatic spiciness enlivens heavy food, so it is a must in hearty, robust dishes. It is also especially good with fatty cuts of meat, where its clean taste balances the richness of the meat. Beef and pork and lamb casseroles would not be the same without it and it is an essential flavouring in many classic meat, game and poultry dishes.

• Infuse sprigs of thyme in oil and wine or vinegar to be used in salad dressings or marinades for meat and fish.

• Slow-cooked dishes, such as French cassoulets and daubes, are all flavoured with thyme. Examples include *boeuf à la bourguignonne, coq au vin and pintade* (guinea fowl) *en daube.*

• Traditional British dishes are often flavoured with thyme, too, notably faggots, liver and onions, pork sausages, game stews, oxtail, boiled bacon, steak and kidney pudding and Lancashire hotpot.

• Thyme is often added to Irish stew.

• Carrot and thyme soup is a sensational combination.

• Experiment with thyme and fish, either sprinkling it on to fish before grilling or tucking a sprig into salmon or sardines before grilling.

Did you know...?

• In the past, thyme was used to cure chills, coughs and colds, to relieve headaches, cramp and colic and to help sleeplessness or loss of appetite in children.

• Essential oil of thyme (thymol), is a strong antiseptic; an infusion can be used as a gargle.

• Thyme can be drunk as a tea, but it is important to be aware that it is a strong diuretic.

Serves 4

Preparation 15 mins

Cooking 1 hr

Calories 236

Fat 9g

1 tbsp vegetable oil
1 small red pepper and
1 small green pepper,
deseeded and thinly sliced
1 onion, thinly sliced
5cm (2in) piece of fresh root
ginger, finely chopped
2 garlic cloves, crushed
2 tbsp garam masala
or Schwartz Medium Bombay
Crushed Curry Spices
1 tsp each paprika, turmeric
and chilli powder
4 cardamom pods, crushed
Good pinch of salt
8 skinless boneless chicken
thighs, cut into 4 pieces
200g tub Greek yogurt
400g can chopped tomatoes
Fresh coriander, to garnish

Chicken rogan josh

1 Heat the oil in a large heavy-based frying pan.
Add the peppers, onion, ginger, garlic, spices and
salt. Fry over a low heat for 5 minutes until the
peppers and onion have softened. Add the chicken
and 2 tablespoons of yogurt. Increase the heat to
medium and cook for 4 minutes until the yogurt is
absorbed. Repeat with the remaining yogurt.

2 Increase the heat to high, add the tomatoes and
200ml (7fl oz) of water and bring to the boil. Reduce
the heat, cover and simmer for 30 minutes, until the
chicken is tender, stirring occasionally. Add water if
the sauce becomes too dry. Uncover, turn the heat
to high and cook, stirring constantly, for 5 minutes
until the sauce thickens. Garnish with coriander.

turmeric

Also known as Indian saffron because of the colour it lends to dishes, turmeric is a versatile and traditional spice. Turmeric is a key ingredient of many Indian dishes for its unique bright yellow colour, its peppery aroma and musky flavour.

Turmeric is the thick, cylindrical rhizome, or underground stem, of a tropical plant related to ginger. Although sometimes compared to saffron, it has a very different flavour – more musky, slightly peppery, with a hint of ginger. Mixed with other ingredients, it has a balancing and enhancing effect. Turmeric is most commonly available in ground form. Added to cooking oil before the main ingredient, turmeric has a more pungent taste; if added after, it lends a more subtle flavour.

Culinary uses

Turmeric gives colour and flavour to curries, vegetarian dishes, pilau rice, fish, eggs, pickles, chutneys, cream sauces and butter sauces.

• Turmeric is used in nearly every Indian meat, lentil and vegetable dish. It is also a good preservative and is used for pickles and chutneys.

• Seafood sauces can be enriched with turmeric.

Did you know...?

• Traditionally, turmeric paste was taken as a tonic to purify blood. It was also believed to help clear sinuses and was even used to treat skin conditions.

• Turmeric is considered to be a sacred spice by Hindus.

vanilla

Used for centuries by the Aztecs to flavour chocolate, this fragrant, exotic, slender, black seedpod with its sweet, smoky aroma and distinct taste is one of the world's most favourite flavourings for sweet dishes such as custards and ice creams.

Vanilla is the seedpod of a perennial creeper or vine belonging to the orchid family that grows in the tropics. Vanilla pods are picked when they're still green and have no scent. The lengthy curing process, which develops vanilla's fragrant aroma, is one reason for its high cost. The best cured pods are dark brown, narrow and long, and have a wrinkled skin. The pods should be fairly supple. Inside are slightly sticky, tiny black seeds, which can be extracted from the pod to add extra flavour to many sweet dishes. There are many ways to extract the flavour from the pods, one being to store two or three pods in a jar of sugar; this flavours the sugar and helps retain the flavour of the pods. Good-quality vanilla pods give an even better flavour than vanilla essence and can be reused many times – even after warming and steeping in milks and sauces – if they are washed and dried well after use. A good-quality vanilla pod will keep its flavour for many months.

Culinary uses

Vanilla complements cakes, puddings, cream, ice cream, rice puddings, pancakes and custard. It also has a special affinity with chocolate.

- For sauces, custards and ice cream, infuse the milk with a vanilla pod. The same method can be used for syrups and poached fruit.

Serves 4

Preparation 20 mins plus
15 mins cooling time

Cooking 8 mins

Calories 209

Fat 6g

675g (1lb 8oz) mixed summer
berries, defrosted if frozen

75ml (3fl oz) port

50g (2oz) caster sugar

2 strips orange rind

Juice of 1 orange

1 tsp ground mixed spice

For the vanilla yogurt

1 vanilla pod, split

200g tub Greek yogurt

1 tbsp clear honey

Red fruits & vanilla yogurt

1 To make the vanilla yogurt, scrape the seeds
from the vanilla pod into the yogurt and stir in the
honey. Cover and refrigerate.

2 Clean and hull the berries, if necessary. Put the
berries into a saucepan with the port, sugar, orange
rind and juice and the mixed spice. Gently heat for
5–8 minutes, until the fruit is just softened.

3 Remove the saucepan from the heat and set
aside for 15 minutes to cool slightly. Serve the still-
warm fruits with a spoonful of vanilla yogurt.

index

Aïoli 38
allspice **6–7**
antiseptic 72
aphrodisiac 51
apples 24, 28, 42
Apricot & lamb kebabs **29**
aubergines 10, 52

Baharat 28
barbecues 62
basil **8–11,** 58
bay leaf **12–13,** 71
beans 31, 52
béchamel sauce 51, 55, 61
beef 23, 42, 51, 72
  boeuf à la bourguignonne 72
  casserole 24
  Cottage (or clapshot) pie **59**
  minced 12
  stew, spiced Spanish **7**
biscuits 23, 24, 28, 41
blood 38, 75
bolognese sauce 12, 51
bouillabaisse 34, 64
bouquet garni 12, 56, 58, 71
bourride 34
bread pudding, lemony **50**
breads 14, 26, 31, 35, 41
  garlic bread 10, 38
breath, freshening 14, 15, 34,
  36, 58, 67

Cabbage 14
cakes 14, 23, 24, 28, 41, 42,
  64, 76
caraway seed **14**
cardamom **15, 28**

carrots 14
  Carrot & orange soup **28**
  carrot & thyme soup 72
  Cumin-spiced carrot soup **30**
casseroles 12, 23, 24, 38, 61,
  71, 72
  cassoulet 72
  chicken 55
  winter sausage 70
cayenne pepper 18
cheese 10, 14, 18, 31, 32, 45,
  51, 52, 55, 56, 67, 72
chicken 26, 31, 32, 45, 52,
  55, 56, 62, 64, 68, 71, 72
  coq au vin 72
  poulet à l'estragon 68
  roast 42
  rogan josh **74**
  Spanish chicken & chorizo **54**
  Stir-fry noodles & **40**
chillies 6,16–19, 26, 28, 39, 55
  chilli con carne 18, 31
  Chilli-spiked mussels with
  spaghetti **39**
chives **20–1**
chocolate 23, 76
cholesterol 38
chorizo & chicken, Spanish **54**
chutneys 26, 28, 35, 48, 75
cinnamon **22–3,** 28
circulation 41, 58
cloves **24–5,** 28
colds 17, 41, 46, 72
coleslaw 14, 32
colic 72
constipation 9
cooling properties 15, 17

coriander leaf **26–7**
coriander seed **28–9**
Cottage (or clapshot) pie **59**
coughs 72
couscous 16, 31, 41
crumbles 6, 22, 28, 42
cumin seed 28, **30–1**
Cumin-spiced carrot
  soup **30**
curries 6, 15, 18, 23, 26, 28,
  31, 34, 35, 41, 64, 75
custards 62, 76

Daube 72
depression 17
dhal 31, 35
diarrhoea 6, 35
digestive aids 12, 15, 17, 34,
  35, 38, 46, 51, 58, 67
Dill-crusted salmon **33**
dill weed **32–3**
dolmades 48
duck 62, 67
dumplings 14

Eggs 10, 18, 20, 32, 45, 52,
  55, 56, 67, 68, 72, 75

Faggots 72
falafel 31
fatigue 67
fattoush 58
fennel seed **34,** 36
fenugreek **35**
fines herbes 20, 58
fish 10, 20, 21, 26, 32, 34, 38,
  41, 45, 48, 52, 58, 62, 64,

68, 72, 75
smoked 20
soups and stews 34, 55, 64
flatulence 6, 35, 38
fruit salads 15, 48, 62

Gall bladder 58
game 42, 62, 67, 72
gammon 24
garam masala 23, 28, 31
garlic 6, 10, **36–9,** 58, 67
gazpacho 10
ginger **40–1**
goulash 14, 55
gravadlax 32
gums, bleeding 67

Haddock & chive butter
   sauce **21**
hair tonic 35
ham 56
   roast, with cloves **25**
harissa sauce 18
hazelnut crumble,
   peach & **22**
headaches 9, 15, 72
hollandaise sauce 68

Ice cream 76
immune system 38, 72
impotency 15
insomnia 9, 51, 72
Irish stew 72
Irish whiskey 24
iron 58

Juniper berries **42**

Kebabs, lamb & apricot **29**
kidneys 24, 58, 72

Lamb 28, 31, 45, 46, 48, 52,
   56, 62, 68, 72
   & apricot kebabs **29**
   chops 10, 20
   roast 28, 38, 46, 62
Lancashire hotpot 72
lassi 28
lemongrass **43**
Lemony bread pudding **50**
lentils 28, 31, 58, 75
liver & onions 72

Mace 50–1
mackerel 34
marjoram **44–5,** 52, 71
mayonnaise 38, 55, 68
milk puddings 12, 45, 51
minestrone 67
mint **46–9,** 58
mixed herbs 45
mulled wine 23, 24
muscular aches and pains 12
mushrooms
   garlic 58
   Mushroom pizza **44**
mussels, chilli-spiked, with
   spaghetti **39**

Nervous tension 9
nutmeg 28, **50–1**

Omelettes 20, 32, 68
orange
   & carrot soup **28**
   pan-fried pork with **66**
oregano **52–3**

Pan-fried pork with orange **66**
paprika 28, **54–5**
parsley 36, **56–9,** 71

pasta 38, 51, 52, 58, 71
   Chilli-spiked mussels with
   spaghetti **39**
   & spicy tomato sauce **13**
   Stortelli & sweet peppers **53**
Peach & hazelnut crumble **22**
peas 46
pepper **60–1**
perfumes 6, 24
pesto 10, 26
pickling spice 6
pizzas 38, **44,** 52
pork 14, 23, 28, 42, 45, 52,
   55, 62, 67, 71, 72
   pan-fried, with orange **66**
potatoes 14, 20, 32, 46, 51,
   55, 62, 64
   Cottage (or clapshot) pie **59**
   jacket 20
   potato salad 20, 34, 58
   roast, grilled or fried 62
   rösti 55
prawns, garlic & parsley 58

Quiches 32

Rabbit 48, 72
raita 26, 48
Red fruits & vanilla yogurt **77**
red pepper 18
remoulade sauce 68
rheumatism 58, 67
rhubarb 28
rice 23, 24, 26, 31
   dolmades 48
   pilau 75
   pudding 12, 76
risotto 34
Roast ham with cloves **25**
Roasted shallots with

rosemary **63**
rogan josh, chicken **74**
rosemary **62–3**
rösti **55**
rouille 38, 64

Saffron **64–5**
sage 45, **66–7**, 71
salads 20, 32, 38, 45, 56, 58,
    67, 68
    fattoush 58
    tomato & mozzarella 10
    potato 20, 34, 58
    tabbouleh **47, 48**
salmon 34
    Dill-crusted **33**
    gravadlax 32
    grilled 6
    smoked 61
sambhar powder 35
satay 18
sauces
    béarnaise 68
    béchamel 51, 55, 61
    Bolognese 12, 51
    chive butter **21**
    harissa 18
    hollandaise 68
    Mexican salsa 26
    mint **48**
    parsley **56-8**
    parsley butter 58
    remoulade 68
    spicy tomato, pasta & **13**
    tartare 68
sauerkraut 14, 42
sausage casserole, winter **70**
seed cake 14
shallots, roasted, with
    rosemary **63**

sickness 41
sinuses, blocked 75
skin problems 75
sore throats 9, 46, 67
soups 12, 32, 38, 61
    bean 31
    carrot 28, **30,** 72
    fish 34
    gazpacho 10
    minestrone 67
    spinach 51
spaghetti, chilli-spiked mussels
    with **39**
Spanish chicken & chorizo **54**
Spiced Spanish beef stew **7**
Spicy vegetable couscous **16**
spinach 23, 28, 51
steak 20
    au poivre **60**
    & kidney 24, 72
stews 12, 15, 38, 41, 61, 71
    fish 55
    goulash 55
    Irish 72
    spiced Spanish beef **7**
    vegetable 31
stir-fries 18, 41
    noodles & chicken **40**
Stortelli & sweet peppers **53**
stuffing 26, 42, 52, 67, 71
Summer tabbouleh **47**
sweet peppers 10, 52, 55
    stortelli & **53**

Tabbouleh, Summer **47**
tarragon **68–9**
tartare sauce 68
thyme 45, **70–3**
toasts
    cinnamon 23

Tomato & basil **8**
tomatoes 9–10, 18, 26, 48, 51,
    52, 67
Tomato & basil toasts **8**
tomato & mozzarella salad 10
tomato salsa 26
tomato sauce **13,** 45, 62
toothache 24
tuna au poivre 61
turkey **72**
    & tarragon sauce **69**
turmeric **74–5**

Vanilla **76–7**
    yogurt, red fruits & **77**
veal 45, 48, 51, 55, 67, 68
venison 42
vodka, spiced 42

Wasp stings 9
Winter sausage casserole **70**

Yogurt 64
    raita 26, 48
    Red fruits & vanilla **77**

picture credits
Howard Shooter: cover;
plus herb & spice pictures
Philip Wilkins:
    7, 8, 16, 29, 53, 54.
Frank Weider: 13, 44, 47.
Jean Cazals: 21.
Thomas Odulate: 22, 33, 70.
Laurie Evans:
    25, 60, 66, 69, 74.
Christine Hanscomb:
    30, 39,50, 63, 77.
Peter Cassidy: 59.